STAINED WITH THE COLOURS OF SUNDAY MORNING

STAINED WITH THE COLOURS OF SUNDAY MORNING

POEMS BY
RAYANNE HAINES

inanna poetry & fiction series

INANNA Publications and Education Inc.
Toronto, Canada

The publisher gratefully acknowledges the support of the Canada Council for the Arts and the Ontario Arts Council for its publishing program. The publisher is also grateful for the financial assistance received from the Government of Canada..

Cover design: Val Fullard

Library and Archives Canada Cataloguing in Publication

Haines, Rayanne, 1973–, author
         Stained with the colours of Sunday morning / Rayanne Haines.

(Inanna poetry & fiction series)
Poems.
Issued in print and electronic formats.
ISBN 978–1–77133–525–6 (softcover).— ISBN 978–1–77133–526–3 (epub).—
ISBN 978–1–77133–527–0 (Kindle).— ISBN 978–1–77133–528–7 (pdf)

        I. Title. II. Series: Inanna poetry and fiction series

PS8615.A3852S73 2018   C811'.6   C2018–901541–1
                                                                        C2018–901542–X

Printed and bound in Canada

Inanna Publications and Education Inc.
210 Founders College, York University
4700 Keele Street, Toronto, Ontario M3J 1P3 Canada
Telephone: (416) 736–5356   Fax (416) 736–5765
Email: inanna.publications@inanna.ca Website: www.inanna.ca

MIX
Paper from
responsible sources
FSC® C004071

For the mothers —
all of you

Contents

III. Siamo pieni dei colori della vita che abbiamo costruito, 1988-2013

IV. Quando anche le ombre piegano le loro ginocchia, 2014

Isabella Caro – 1944 to 2014
Alina Caro – 1967 to present
Georgia Caro – 1994 to present
Giorgio Caro – 1940 to present

Eravamo ragazze italiane, Unbound
1944-1974

How to tell heart stories – *Georgia*

Mia Nonna taught me how to fall in love.
She taught me to tell heart stories.

My Grandmother's life was song.
Her music made men weep.
Her story told through 10,000 steps
on the streets of Firenze, floating naked
in the Black Sea, painting her skin
with the spices of Bombai, drinking
red wine from the bottle in Paris.

Vero Amore, she would say,
dances in the street in the evening air,
forgives with the rise and fall of the moon.

Vero Amore, she would say,
are fingers covered in flour, a tattered apron,
the kiss of cherries on your child's chin.

My Grandmother's hair hung to her waist.
Grandfather would pause to inhale whenever
she was close.   Stand bewitched.

Even then, when their love had aged,
his fingers would curl with the memory
of getting lost in the scent. Her hair
smelled like cinnamon and the coffee cake
she baked every Sunday morning.

Adorare Vita Bambina she would say,
as she kneaded the dough.
This is love.

Footsteps – *Isabella*

I was born to the sounds of German soldiers
as they marched out of our city.
Ma Famiglia rejoiced in that departure
as much as my hardy cries.

Salvage became my inheritance, my birth story.
I was the daughter of survivors. The daughter who
would rebuild a better Italia, a stronger Italia.

The first songs sung to me
were freedom songs. Lullabies
about heroes pulled apart in shadows.

Resistance tales of dragons
forged from iron and steel.
My first steps those of a warrior
in stride with my mother

to spit on the graves of our oppressors.
No room for soft girls in my world.
We were born severe women
to reclaim our country, alongside our men.

I was born to the march of deliverance. My heart's
first beats, matched by its staccato.
I was raised to the rhythm of hunger
for more — to take
back.

Wings – *Isabella*

I should have been born a raven.
To cry out – *Tomorrow*
while I flew above the clouds.
Wings turned black
from being born to battle's sorrow.

When I fell in love it was a storm.
We were insanity. Lust of Ravens'
legend. Black as night, fiercely joined —
never caring how high we flew.

But when I conceived, I bequeathed
wings of white to my child.
No battle scars forced upon her.
We would flourish
beyond the reach of our sins.

The Art of Growing Up Italian – *Isabella*

We were scandalous, almost foreign —
to lounge blithely beside the River Arno.
Our pink mopeds blocking paths.
Our young legs bared to disapproving eyes.

All around men in sombre suits
rushed back and forth, heady with responsibility.
Women in woollen scarves,
hands locked on careless children
scolded, *take heed, keep your knees clean.*

Intoxicated with independence,
we rolled in the grass,
as though it were an unmade bed.
Expectation and decision forgotten.
Our futures planned on a whim.

Laughter our sole consideration.
Rules and moral obligations
would not shape us, we swore.
We were Italian girls — Unbound.

Brushstrokes – *Isabella*

Men pleaded to paint my skin; Smudge
the small of my back with their fingertips.

So I let them touch me, abandoned myself
to passion, flirted and flittered through notebooks.

They would beseech me to run away;
Tell me tales of how they would
build me a castle, make me a princess.

But I'd rather be a wanderer than waited on.
Would rather write of mythic sirens than childhood fairytales.

No, No. I'm not ready to love you yet, I'd tell them.
And then I'd swing my hips and allow them to kiss me.

Spices – *Isabella*

My skin carries the spices
of men I've made love to.
There were not so many men.
But that depends on who you are asking.

There is liberty in sex play.
Sweat from two lovers lingering
in the room, long after they are gone.
Pillows hold the memories
of bodies breathing into one another.

I would not shower after I left them.
Primal — I lay on the bed
to absorb them.

Questions Run Like Rivers – *Isabella*

Lovers scratch the back of my neck
with phantom fingers. Inhale my musk
as they stalk me. Envision
muscled calves wrapped
around their waist – hands gripped
tight in silence, or in those loud moments
when silence roars.

My voice becomes whisper.
A rasp. A heathen's growl.
They think this matters,
this sound lays claim.

Questions run like rivers through
my veins. Answers, the aphrodisiac.
It is the unknowing that pulls
me. Beasts of legend,
Gods of mythology, Goddesses imbued with power.
It is the story of the feminine that draws me,
the pen of Oracles I crave.

I regret nothing. Not
the raking of bodies back and forth. Not
the nights I lay still. Not
waiting for after to begin.

I lay unclaimed — traced
a path while staring at stars.
Connected it to the river of lines
on my hands.
Followed its current.

The Innocent – *Isabella*

Historians tell me Italia lost
her soul in the second world war.

In the old country the war
is remembered in ceremonies,
monuments, museums, in cemeteries.

We are reminded — sons and soldiers
were killed in combat
they did not choose.
Thousands of Italian Jews
buried in concentration camps.
Italian civilians executed
for parts played in resistance.

We are reminded
we followed a madman;
We followed two mad men.

My mother will say she lived it —
neighbours betrayed neighbours,
then sheltered them after they
hung a monster in the square.

Swimming with Mermaids – *Isabella*

In the Sardinian Sea,
you forget the feel of earth.

Life an endless wave,
bodies shaped by current.

No above or below, only
the movement of water over skin.

The ocean christens you on her
breast milk, salt her elixir.

The sun reflects diamonds, held in trust
by mermaids at the bottom of the sea.

This Is How We Began – *Isabella*

Forthright and impertinent.
Books in my bloodstream.
Faded pages my constant companions.
            Nights filled with wine and impudence.

You had more significant things to do
than speak with self–important school girls.
They called you Giorgio
respect in their voices,
I stared across the room, unabashed.
Green eyes scored violet.

That first night you pressed
my body against a stone wall —
sinning on my mind. Whispered, *mine*
against the heartbeat at my throat
before you strode away.

Your world was one of
concrete details and work
that broke the backs of lesser men.
Your young face already
marked with laugh lines.
            You smelled of whiskey
            tobacco, horse flesh.

Months later, our bodies
sprawled against a willow tree,
university books forgotten under
asiago cheese and sangiovese grapes,
I told you I was ready to fall in love.
You laughed, *right where we are?*
Before you leaned in and hummed
a love song along my lips.

The Canals of Venice – *Isabella*

My body bends like light reflecting off the moon.
Undulates in the sway of sounds rippling around us.
Sweats in tune with the river's flow.

Hands above head, hips thrust, back arched.
We didn't start this for a gentle love story.
Our love is red, fire walking.

Two panthers fighting for the right to own our skin.
Sleek and oiled, getting off on the high
of each other's scent.

I test the limitations of flesh and flame.
Melt against fever built in moments of trust.
Pitch and strain under hands that sweep inhibitions.

Whispers crawl along my neck,
Tu sei la vita, sei il respiro
You are life, you are breath.

A Wedding Vow – *Isabella*

Be alive with me
in this ocean that is my body.
Keep me from drowning in expectation.
Be a wave with me.

Don't ask the wild women heart of me to bend
to you like flower petals. This I save
for nights when moonlight and wine are mine alone.
I do not need to light this village with love, just
a soft glow in the corner of the room.

Get drunk with me,
on these grapes from your father's fields.
Let's stain our feet dancing, wash
our hair in Chianti. Guzzle it.

I offer you days of madness
and inhibition, fits of brilliance, days when I
am lost in books and silence. I offer you
my hands in your hair, stories of fire
in your ear, nights starring at our children.

I offer you my spine — strong enough to carry the weight
of shadows to come our way. I offer you

wild dreams and uncompromising reality. I give you
the life growing within my body.

Say it is always you and I, hands clasped against
those who would burn us down,
and I am yours, forever.

There Was No Name for it Back Then – *Isabella*

I couldn't name her for a week.
The name had to be worthy
of who she would become.

Her father's large hands could enclose
her body. He held her pink skin
against his caramel; nuzzled
her downy head, laughed at my scattered look.

You will give yourself wrinkles, my love.
This should not be so difficult. Come, hold her.
Her heartbeat will tell you her name.

I couldn't hold her for eight days.
The nurses shook their heads at me.
Her grandmothers shamed
by my failure.

You will leave her be.
She will come to it when she is able,
I heard my husband scold them
on the fourth day of our daughter's life.
And they would listen, of course,

scramble to do as they were told.
My daughter and I would never bend
to another's will, I told myself
as I lay in the hospital bed,
unable to embrace her.

On the eighth day of her life he came to me.
You will hold your daughter now,
You have named her for light.
Do not show her weakness.

He softened his command
by stroking my hair back from my face
before resting her on my chest.

I cried as she suckled
at my breast. My milk dried up,
my emptiness displayed to all.

I was unclean, ungrateful,
the women in my family reminded me
when my husband wasn't near,
as another fed my child,

crooned her name.

An Emptiness – *Isabella*

I was a raindrop in a thunderstorm, lost
to the whim of some deception.
I hadn't counted on not being in control —
on the rebellion of my ovaries.

I wondered how I had failed.
Was it a penance for
being loved too well? Did I
have to learn more about sacrifice?

I was a black sky, waiting for morning.
Still, I took solace in shadows,
so as not to see a husband
who understood — who also grieved.

This was the weight I bore,
         what my womb refused him.
I could not kiss his mouth
without anger, without
loss, guilt, and
in those small moments — relief.

My Husband – *Isabella*

1

Giorgio kissed me goodbye in the departure lounge.
His kiss tasted like the earth.
His hands kneaded my shoulders.

Always his hands were rough, worn.
His character shone in the dark green of his eyes.
A spirit stronger than mine — deeper.

Let me be clear.
I have never loved another.
Giorgio was my home.

I envied the peace
he found in everyday things.
The symbiotic energy he shared with the land,

while I flew above it. Never clear
how to come down, without
feeling like I had fallen.

My Husband – *Isabella*

2

I betrayed him once —
After that airport kiss.
That kiss that felt like it was
too much for my flighty heart.

I sought Dionysus.
Lied to that lover as I lied to myself;
that in this, love did not matter.

That taking another body into mine
released my wings. I told myself I

was above it. On different soil I
could be innocent — this was freedom.

Crushed under another,
I did not soar above the clouds, weightless.
Only echoed.

After — broken, heaving —
I stumbled, pretending I
had not cut my wings.

Shattered: stripped myself raw.

My Husband – *Isabella*

3

Giorgio met me at the gate,
to welcome his woman home.
He knew what I had done when he saw me.
I watched his step falter a moment,
as he walked toward me.

He kissed me deeper that night;
Loved me harder. Branded me with the musk
of the earth he was such a part of.
In his loving, I wept my sins.

He tasted the salt of them. Maybe
to take the pain of it into himself, to release
me from the burden of it.

We never spoke of the betrayal.
My quiet farmer
sat with me to stare at sunsets,
bragged of me to his friends,

fought with more passion,
laughed with more lust.
loved with no hesitation,
no quarter.

Every step thereafter
we took in tandem. Every

choice made together.
I grew roots —solid, sure, rich.

That summer, his skin weathered,
marked by wind and sun.
His auburn hair grew long and shaggy.
His muscles took on a leanness — rugged and fierce.

I watched him wander through our days.
In awe at how field hands
deferred to him in all things. Studied him

training a foal, grew full
with yearning, watched hands gentle,
yet firm on the filly's flesh.
And always they would bend to him.

He demanded release from my body.
And I, pliant, fevered
would give him all he asked.

Saying Goodbye to my Country – *Isabella*

Giorgio's pride was unwavering
when I was offered a professorship in Canada.
This is what lovers did, he promised me.
Ma Bella, Only thirty and offered such a position!

We spent the evenings locked in laughter.
Downed fine whiskey as we poured
over plans. Stripped naked and fed each other
dates as we celebrated.

I made short work of goodbyes
to friends who'd always known I'd leave.
Disregarded my daughter's concerns.
Ignored censorious family frowns.

I greeted each day with relish,
took long walks along the rivers,
rode my bicycle to visit old haunts,
returned library books held onto for years.

Spent days sipping cappuccino in the park,
falling back in love with Italia.
So that when I left her, I would remember
how she raised me.

Cercando di far ombra ai fantasmi
in una casa di luce
1974-1988

not gently to love – *Alina*

my mother told me I was
conceived in venice
in the alley of a baker

the gondola shepherds
cry for the flock of tourists
loud in the background

the conceivement was a hurried thing
a knowing need to take each other
both unwilling to wait

for the sacrament of marriage
she tells me she felt
the quickening in her belly

a capturing in her womb
a daughter, she told my father
and they were joyous

my mother told me
they were married in tuscany
in the field of a farmer

she told me this before I left the first time
made me promise to search for the same
a promise I trod under my feet

my mother left me
in a cradle in florence
in the care of a relative

her pursuit of herself
of something more
disguised as seeking knowledge

my mother's love
always left me behind

for a walk that was not mine – *Alina*

thankfully my mother married
a wealthy man   a man taken
with her lust for adventure

each time she wandered
he would kiss her neck
wrap his arms around her waist

he would say *I shall see you soon*
go learn something new

when she was offered a position
as a professor they were ecstatic
it would be another re–birth
a new life

she never thought her child
would wish to remain in italia
had no interest in a foreign country
she never thought to ask

father would brag *A doctor*
of mythology   a big university

A mythology that offered no hour for me
        barren goddesses worshiped
in place of her child

When Winter Came – *Isabella*

Giorgio wore a look of stupendous
disbelief when we walked out
of the airport into frigid air
of our new country. Like goslings
following their mother, we
followed the university guide.

Our residence was drafty
and cramped. Giorgio declared
he would buy a new home.
My daughter, curled on his lap,
stared at him with worshipful eyes.
Glared back at me.

We spent the night huddled
in a bed. Her arms and legs
strewn across us.
I received the butt end.
Her mahogany locks
rested against Giorgio's cheeks.

Broken Cold – *Isabella*

Barren for days,
months wrapped in ice flow.

Trees turned to bone —
brittle. That sacred den

of re–birth, hidden.
We wondered if the earth

was trying to finish herself off.
Each February was the same.

Our bodies desperate
for the lush wine blood of the sea.

When Spring Came – *Isabella*

we bought land outside
the city. Giorgio made plans
to bring studs from Italy.

Alina was speaking fluent
English, had created fearless friendships.
Still, she glowered — defiant
in distaste for the journey.
My angry daughter, unreachable by me.

This new life
would change things, I was sure.
We had a new beginning. The chains
of the old world would not reach us.
There were no monuments to re–build,
no heroes to sacrifice for.

By another winter she
would look at me with love.

Immigrant – *Isabella*

We missed age — that deep stirring
oldness. The beauty of cities swollen
with old women's stories. Reminders
that we are small.

We became two worlds
trying to find our futures
carved on a cliff edge.

This country — vast, raw. So new
when we put our ear to earth
we could hear the echo
of the spirit bears.

Only One – *Isabella*

I did not bend a knee to Goddess Latona.
Refused to beg for what could not be.

Rather I would dance with my hatchling
in flight. Sing of mythic delights,
discuss the canopies of intellect,
become a congress of three.

She was Light — our Sun, at war
with her own sorrow. This battle,
this passion, grief, a gift from Odin.
Beloved and immeasurable, she carried
the power to lift me off this earth.

in Canada my mother flourished – *Alina*

there were fewer watchful eyes
more freedom for my parents
more laughter from mother

especially in winter
when we bunched together
to keep warm

father would blow
on our hands
try to start finger fires

i could almost love her then
when the three of us
sat with our fingers entwined

i could almost feel
that she wanted me

Moon Lullabies – *Isabella*

Laughter leaked out her body
when she slept. Eyes closed to darkness
she would breathe in sun;
bloom, petals opening.

Head tilted as if listening
to ghosts sing lullabies.
All her angles, soft.
Her jawbone weightless.

I would stroke her hair, crawl silent
into bed. Wish for a different
daylight, where the air didn't choke
all we should have said.

I think I was a better mother
in her dreams. That she returned
home to me there. Dreamed of
white birds flying south.

Such a burden for a young soul.
To have to wait for the sun to go down
before she could love her mother.

she should have known better – *Alina*

after i turned ten
i spent every august
in italia   something about
she should spread her wings

strange   the wisdom
of my mother   Unable to see
how those absent months
desiccated us   how i came
home cracked   fractured
how the pain of those
left behind was a weight
i was too fragile to carry

my soul aged like the leather
on my suitcase   worn down
from too many trips breathing
broken air

she should have known better
returned with me
shouldn't have left me
to suffocate in metal birds
to drown on parched ground

grey – *Alina*

i was in italy when they
told me of my mother's sin
a particularly humid summer
       one in which i would rather
have remained in canada

a last attempt to regain
control by a family forgotten
like faded parchment

how simple to persecute her failings
self–righteous as I was
relentless on behalf
of disregarded ancestors

their grief leaked
from lips   looking for
comfort from a child
a vessel for their loss
damaged more by their need
to seethe than by anything
my mother had done

i returned home grey
carved open by their
destructive whispers

she welcomed me at arrivals
knew that I knew
when she saw my face

i watched her stumble
a moment   The only
indication she ever gave
of my knowing   of her old agony

she held me in her arms
despite my defiance
          and wearing sorrow's mark
my wings turn black
I allowed her

undone – *Alina*

we became silent inhabitants
        submerged in that night

there we were
        trying to shed ghosts
in a house of light

future sentenced by history
        tormented by absent lips

ancient – *Alina*

i wore flesh too young
for my ancient bones
covered with layers
of pink youth   hiding
the resentment of ages

if only i
could grind this
primordial skeleton
take new form
under my skin

shed myself
from the inside out
leave this carcass
for vultures

Origin – *Isabella*

Remorse rested like a shadow
on my spine, until I shed it
like molting feathers.

Insecurity cocooned, burrowed.
Colors the wrong shade,
Rough texture against skin.

Guilt became a language I spoke.
Heavy, guttural, foreign
unknown by gods

The strength of her aversion
cut like glass through
every line of her flesh.

I stalked her strategically,
forced this small peace upon her.
Called Ravens to my aid.

There was no outrunning our ghosts.
Only offering light in place
of haunting things.

questioning birds – *Alina*

in italy my grandmother
had two canaries
housed in separate cages
so they would sing to the other

their music   her church
revered behind bars

released only occasionally
from their shackles
for a brief taste of flight

i never understood
why they let themselves
be controlled   confined

why they did not rebel
        remain silent in protest.

sunday mornings we went to art classes – *Alina*

while father worked
in the barn mother had
me study Michelangelo
Da Vinci, Donatello, Botticelli, Raphael

while father trained
the horses   mother and i
practiced techniques of Rousseau
Monet, Cezanne, Munch, Picasso

mother's hands awkward
with the brushes   mine
soft and elegant — a natural
our instructor assured her
together we revelled
in color and texture   until
i outgrew her

still mother drove
me to my classes
marked her papers while i
found sanctuary in
my practice   soon my
hands became stained
with the colours of sunday mornings

it was sunday morning
when i was accepted
to the art institute of chicago
i remember staring
at the ink on my
mother's shaking fingers
as she read the letter
a second time
how it matched the
dye of paint on mine

Claiming a Future – *Isabella*

On this day of her life
she wore a purple pantsuit under her blue gown.
Mahogany hair draped to her waist
underneath a perfectly positioned cap.

Slight curves hidden under a gown that signified
the entry to adulthood, the leaving behind of youth,
the start of newly chosen things.

Beside me Giorgio released shaky breaths.
His tears made manifest in sweaty palms.
Mine fell from eyes stained the same color as hers.

I watched her walk across the stage
to claim her future, to wield her diploma
like a torch, to rejoin the assembled throng as Bellona.

Afterwards we searched for her
in the horde of parents searching for their own.
Giorgio reached her first;
Encased her in a hug. His booming
voice declaring her superiority.
English forgotten in that moment.
Italian ringing through the hall.

Insecurity and longing lay in my hug
like a first day of school friendship.
Sadness sat with pleasure, missing her,
remembering new beginnings.

*Siamo pieni dei colori della vita
che abbiamo costruito*
1988-2013

no promise – *Alina*

he was made up of small words
no   yes   maybe   if only

until we kissed
our kiss sounded bigger than that
now   tomorrow   always   this time

each kiss   another promise
each kiss   another word
each kiss   another promise
each kiss   another promise
each kiss   another promise

until he ran out of words

desperate to reclaim his voice
i misplaced myself   wore his skin
waged war to keep him

to fulfill the promise
growing in my womb

his body was made up
of harsh words
can't   too hard   not mine

until I begged for silence
begged for lies

Advice to My Daughter – *Isabella*

When you meet a desperate man
offer him a pail of strawberries first.
See if this will ease the
hunger that gnaws at him.

Offer him solace.
Perhaps your smooth shoulders
will give him strength
to rise from his abyss — Perhaps.

Do not offer him your feet or hands.
Those are precious and he
would not know how
to walk in your place,
curl your fingers around a future.

Do not love a man wearing shadows.
For he will turn on you
with the angle of the sun.

You cannot save him
by giving your heart.
He will only drown you;
attempt to slake his thirst.
Gluttonous in famine.

the birth of my daughter – *Alina*

            saw a stranger
hold my hand
i did not invite
my mother to
attend the birth

my husband was
not in the room
when the child was born
of course   a loss
i couldn't voice

he had no care either
about her name
he would choose
the next child's — the boy's
and so i named her Georgia
for her grandfather

mother and father
arrived after my husband
departed   i could hear
their overbearing italian
chatter down the hall

mother giving instructions
to nurses   father packed down
with gifts and supplies
they were sure I needed

my tired nerves frayed
it was important
for him to provide
for his family   i said
when his absence was questioned

an old war briefly
ravaged her face
before her eyes found
those of my child   grief
exited the room

a meeting of eyes   a heartbeat
father placed his palm
on her shoulder   rested his forehead
on her back   said
Mia Amore we have another goddess

the tiniest fracture
an unknown anguish
i could not touch
replaced as she
considered her granddaughter

This vulnerability   my fathers
head bowed in memory
had me handing her
my daughter   and she
rocked her — crooned her name

Newborn – *Isabella*

Pink–tongued and bald,
a half formed human
full of plump rolls
made for my kiss.
Her squeaking noises,
those of a kitten,
learning to purr
in fits and starts, engineered
to make us worship her.

Sent from the goddess Lucina
she was of the earth,
of growing things,
of sunlight and seedlings —
this fresh life, this granddaughter.

it goes on – *Alina*

nestles in the sweet   soft
home of spongy newborn
skin
voice without language

bites through separation
aches   staggers   drunk
with yearning — the mess
of everyday

it is nothing physical
everything flesh

only false tales house
pretty love
old love
forgiving love

sometimes it is
ruptured   consumed
before it reaches the
ripe   tender age
of timeworn things

leaves you
leaves you
leaves you

with broken wings
memories of flying
with new legs
learning to walk again

There are no girly things – *Georgia*

All my childhood weekends
were spent in the care
of my grandparents.

Nonna would read me fairy tales,
(always altered so it was the princess
who slew the dragon)
while drinking red wine by the fireplace.
My pink legs sprawled across her warm body.
Once she let me have a sip. Told me
back in Italy, children were allowed
wine at the dinner table.
Canadians were so uncivilized.

Other weekends I would
explore her office at the university,
wander through empty halls.
investigating abandoned corridors,
sopping up scattered knowledge.

We never did girly things.
Nonna said there was no such thing.
That we were humans.

When Sunlight Calls You – *Isabella*

First there was that wild sunbeam of stars
shimmering across the room. A puddle of it by
the back door just big enough to dip my toes in.

This afternoon it will be a tsunami,
a wave of fractured beams bouncing off the walls.
The cat will roll in it.

and I will count seconds until I abandon
this world of paper and pen. Become instead
a nymph, naked to the glory of the sun.

finding our resilience – *Alina*

we became an alliance
my mother and i
            accomplices in outwitting
a three–year–old

father had it easy
her playmate   he was
always the recipient
of effortless affection
instant obedience

we had to work for it
still — i resented
her some days   for daring
to occupy my place

i was afraid to admit
that she knew how to mother
when even then
i accused her of
failing as mine

it's a daunting thing
        looking at a lifetime
of almosts   admitting
the darkness you lived
in was only a brief shadow

resenting the innocence
of your child
and the resilience
of your mother

My Nonna was a warrior – *Georgia*

On those nights I cried
for a lost father, she
became Amazon. Refused
admittance to his name. Spit
on the image of him.

Her purpose held us together then,
when mother still wept in the dark.
When nightmares stalked us.

She became Griffin   wings outstretched,
proud, defiant. Building a road map
for my mother's second chance.
Became guardian of my heritage,
of who I was still to be. Gave
me a pen, told me to use it as a sword.

Waiting for Time – *Isabella*

The ocean has much to teach about patience.

It will bring to shore
only what is timely to give. You may
keep these gifts unless
the ocean reclaims. Then you
must lay your body
on the sand in supplication
as you wait.

You will not be content to search
the depths of the sea but once. Swimming
against the tide a useless endeavour.
If you simply watch drift awhile,
you will get where you need to go.

The trees have much to teach about rising.

About standing still as you grasp
for stars. You will find shelter
in their arms. They give it freely, if
you are simply willing to remain
with them a while.

They do not go looking for more.
They have no need. Every season
brings new treasures. All they
have to do is stand tall, raise
their arms to sunbeams,
welcome guests and wait.

In Florence – *Isabella*

I forget the sound of the Arno,
that Siren call, that music of Firenze.

It started as an ache in my belly
for smoking cigarettes in the Piazza del Carmine.

A secret pleading for elegant women —
Espresso in one hand, cannoli in the other.

A missing for the soul of my people,
their ferocious zest for living big.

A desperate declaration for the language
of Italia rolling off refined tongues.

For Florence.

Sunday mornings we baked – *Georgia*

Mia Nonna liked to give advice
when she baked. Simple words
rolled with the flavour of history,
garnished with the color of Italian.

She guided my hand as
I added spices, slowed
the rhythm of my stir. Moved
with measured abandon,
as if each day was savoured.
Those mornings were a jazz song.

Nonna would hum when not talking.
Nonno tapping his foot to her beat.
      A lifetime of love songs.
There was a swagger to the scent of
their home; Old world, with attitude.
Every Sunday, I watched them fall in love again.

Church – *Georgia*

We never went to Church.
Nonno had no time for men of the Cloth.
The horses wouldn't keep
for a prayer   he used to say.

The path to heaven is earth. Deep
black soil, raven black, fertilized
with flesh, musky   we are swimming
knee deep in it. God rests in the

standing talls, the four leggeds, the winged ones.
Spirit voices bellow, if we remember to listen.
The wind whispers stories, passed
from daughter to daughter   from Pagan to Saint.

Sei Tu Amore – *Isabella*

We are filled with the colours of the life we build.
Aromas that swirl around
the infant cradled on our hips.
Soft bread dipped in olive oils and vinaigrettes.

Basil, Garlic, Ricotta
tattooed on our fingertips.

Chianti and Cinnamon, Espresso and Honeybread.
Flavours made to linger on your tongue
whispers against your neck.

i do not live in it – *Alina*

mother said some men
carry stone wombs
too brittle to welcome life
they run from it
        ashes to ashes to dust

a grown woman
i still taste the residue
his leaving left
but I do not live in it

i invented myself
by his absence
nurtured by oil paints
and feminism

learned how to be
one of the growing things
imprinted by wildflowers
and storybooks

when i loved my mother – *Alina*

i watched her silhouette
take shape under the wool
blanket   her hair greyed
and natural   lying loose
about her shoulders

lost in her dreaming
books scattered
around her slight frame
i was struck by
her beauty

quiet   I settled
beside her on the couch
curled my toes next to hers
waited as she raised the blanket
          a silent offering

that day understanding was
an easy thing   A quiet easing
of broken places   of sought
moments   of knowing her.

my head against her
shoulder   she offered me
a sip from her tea cup
its edges chipped   yellow irises
scratched into the.china.
she'd brought this cup from Italy
like she'd brought the rest of us
            offered it a new home

With Age – *Isabella*

How can we find wrinkles sexy?
Our flesh having rebelled long ago?
Maybe this is why we lose our sight as
we age, I laughed at him one night.

Thick eyebrows burrowed,
Your wrinkles are your love songs,
he assured me before covering my mouth with his.

To love so deeply is learned, we discovered.
To love past heartache, past annoyance, past indifference.
To love through indiscretion, through moments of
intentional hurt — when love becomes a way to
challenge the other — when you'd rather hate.

We plant tomatoes together now.
Let our hands find each other under the soil,
our fingers mimicking caresses.
The neighbours offer to help —
They could do it faster and we
could sit in the sun they say —
as they watch us lean on each other
grunting to rise with some semblance
of the grace we used to have.

They do not notice the hand planted firmly
on my buttocks. They do not hear him whisper,
Mia Amore — *I love to see your hair glisten in the sun.*

Olive oil – *Georgia*

Nonna smells like olive oil
when I visit her today.
She rubs it onto her hands.
Tells me our hands speak our histories.
She rubs the oil on her hands, her skin,
to keep the memories fresh.

To remember the stories and hand them on.
Her skin leathered, worn, forgiving.
As tender as the day her mother
showed her how to work the oil in.
She turns her hands over and looks at them,
lost in some recollection. Perhaps remembering
her birth country. Perhaps a friend left behind.

So much life I lived, she says as she studies the hands that cupped
oceans to her mouth.
So many handsome men.
These veins rising up   a living map.
Ero una donna selvaggia
she laughs as she looks up.

Fondly she strokes the back of her hand
on my cheek, takes my palms in hers,
and begins to massage them with olive oil.

my mother told me – *Alina*

she was ill on June 6th
in the prairie sun
on a downtown public patio

the waitress served
pomegranate spritzers
while the heat beat down
on us in humid waves
my hands were sweaty
and I rubbed them on my jeans.
i shouldn't have worn jeans

the top i wore had a photo
of Marilyn Munro smoking
a cigarette on it   ochre paint splashed
across one shoulder   i should
have been dressed differently
to receive news like that

mother was dressed
in a white button down blouse
a lilac cardigan wrapped
around her shoulders
her perfect white bob
floating against her neck
the small diamond on her
wedding ring winking at me

i remember thinking she looked
too good for 70   better than me
with my hair half out of its
elastic and stuck to my face

a motorbike roared past
just when she said the words
          drowned her out so
she had to repeat herself

6 weeks
What Mom
6 weeks

          just those words
stark and dark and sweaty and hot

Who knows why these things happen she said
like we were discussing the menu
before she offered me more wine

and I was so angry at her
for wearing that cardigan
          for always being so damned perfect
for everything we were too late to be

*Quando anche le ombre piegano
le loro ginocchia*
2014

Alla Mia Donna – *Giorgio*

We took shape under
moonlight, under sunlight.
Folded into each other
like braided bread. One fold
then the next, then more.
Our love was simple as time.
The color of veins under skin.

Her wild body crafted with
silk and linen wings.
Her fragrant flesh a
meadow of lilacs and honey.
Lips the taste of springtime,
of snow falling, of life growing.

We loved borderless, ageless.
Gorged on each other
godless, finding sight.
Inside her, lived daylight.

To my woman
even shadows bend their knee.
Without her
I am thin as the edge of egg shell.
I am empty as a fallow wheat field.
Mi Sono Perso.

To live like her – *Georgia*

Maybe it is about living
undone, living unconstrained,
living on the edge of too much.
Maybe we should dance sylph–like,
take a raven's flight.
Inhabit those places where we
drink red wine to welcome sunrise.

I brought a bottle of Chianti
to her funeral. Poured a glass
for Nonno and Mother as
I read her eulogy. Maybe
we should all learn to live like her.

in this room – *Alina*

i cannot think of death
        and her in the same room

not in this room
with its salmon walls
and sterile scent

i want to climb over the wall
into the fragrant garden
and lay her body
next to the raspberry bush

i want to spray her perfume
        have it fall like the northern
lights on our skin

i want it to be winter again
and i am climbing off the plane
overwhelmed and feeling
smaller than an insect

i would rather feel
that   than this being
alone on the earth again

Bread – *Isabella*

I will wither at day's end.
Lost to a devil that wouldn't be beaten.

How strong is hope in the face
of alone? When alone
is what you are left with.

I am still there. In the house
where we kneaded dough.

There is no alone.
I am not alone.

Caro mio

Bake the bread
we love and put it on the
counter. So you can still smell
me in the morning.

Acknowledgements

I would like to thank Alice Major for her mentorship and friendship. Her kind and careful guidance has meant everything to me over the past six years.

Also, gratitude to Kimmy Beach for her insight during the formative stages of writing this collection.

I'd like to sincerely thank Luciana Ricciutelli for giving this collection a home at Inanna Publications.

Thanks to the writers in the trenches, Nichole, Rusti, and Alida for all their thoughtful feedback on my poems. Thank you to Ruthi and Maria for help with the Italian translation.

To my husband, Douglas — my rock, my heart, my own Giorgio; to my children, James and Deen, who I've been desperately in love with since the day they were born; and to my mother–in–law, Maria, whose strength was the inspiration for this collection.

Photo: Rebecca Lippiatt

Rayanne Haines is a bestselling fiction author and award-winning performance poet. She is proud to be the executive director of the Edmonton Poetry Festival. She has had the immense privilege of performing her fiction and poetry for diverse audiences from youth to business professionals, for various reading series, conferences, and festivals. She has been published in anthologies, magazines, and online. Her poetry has been used as the text for the National Youth Choir of Canada, as well as recorded for a United Kingdom talking newspaper for the blind. She's had work published in Canada, the USA, and the UK. *Stained with the Colours of Sunday Morning* is her first full–length poetry collection. She lives in Edmonton.